To:

_____

From:

_____

Date:

_____

YouVersion

Bible Storybook from the Bible App for Kids™

Previously published as *The Bible App for Kids Storybook Bible*.

Copyright © OneHope, 2017.

Text and illustration copyright © 2015 by OneHope, Inc.

The Bible App for Kids™ and YouVersion® are trademarks of Life.Church.

Published in Nashville, Tennessee, by Tommy Nelson. Tommy Nelson is an imprint of Thomas Nelson. Thomas Nelson is a registered trademark of HarperCollins Christian Publishing, Inc.

Tommy Nelson titles may be purchased in bulk for educational, business, fund-raising, or sales promotional use. For information, please e-mail SpecialMarkets@ThomasNelson.com.

**Library of Congress Cataloging-in-Publication Data on file**

ISBN 978-1-4002-1512-6

*Printed in China*

19 20 21 22 23 DSC 6 5 4 3 2 1

**Mfr: DSC / Shenzhen, China / October 2019 / PO #9549952**

# BIBLE STORYBOOK

FROM The Bible App FOR KIDS

Created by YouVersion and OneHope, the *Bible App for Kids* is sharing God's Story with children all around the world. You can interact with all the stories in this book—as well as many others—in the app. Each story comes alive with animation, narration, and music. Download the free *Bible App for Kids* on the App Store, Google Play, and Amazon Appstore, or visit bible.com/kids from your mobile device or tablet.

Tommy NELSON®        YouVersion        OneHope

An Imprint of Thomas Nelson
thomasnelson.com

# CONTENTS

## NEW TESTAMENT

# IN THE BEGINNING

## Creation of the World

GENESIS 1:1-2:4

In the beginning, God made the heavens and the earth. God moved over the darkness and said, "Light!" He called the light "day," and He called the darkness "night."

DAY ONE. DONE!

Then God made a space to separate the waters above from the waters below. He called the space "sky."

## DAY TWO. DONE!

God gathered the waters together, and dry ground appeared. He called the ground "land" and the waters "seas." Then He made plants like grass, grain, and trees.

## DAY THREE. DONE!

Then God made lights in the sky. He made the sun for the day, the moon for the night, and all the stars.

DAY FOUR. DONE!

God made fish to swim in the waters and birds to fly in the sky. "Have babies!" He told them. "Fill the world with splashing and singing."

## DAY FIVE. DONE!

Next, God made animals. He made farm animals, wild animals, and animals that crawl on the ground. "Just one more thing to make," God said. "The most special thing of all."

So, in His image, God made man and woman. "Have babies," He said. "Take charge of the world. Care for the fish, the birds, and the animals."

## DAY SIX. DONE!

Then God looked at everything He had made.
"It's very good!" He said. So on the seventh day,
He rested and made that day special.

## DAY SEVEN. DONE!

What was God's most special creation?

God was very pleased with everything He made. There was no pain or death. Everything was good. Then God gave the first man and woman a rule to obey.

# THE FIRST SIN
## The Fall

GENESIS 3:1-24

The first man and woman, Adam and Eve, lived in a beautiful garden that God made for them. But Satan came as a crafty serpent and tempted Adam and Eve.

15

"Did God say you must not eat the fruit from these trees?" the serpent asked Eve.

"Just the tree in the middle," Eve replied. "If we eat from it, we'll die."

"You won't die!" said the serpent. "There's a reason why God doesn't want you to eat from that tree. If you do, you'll be like Him. You'll know what He knows!"

Eve ate the fruit. She gave some to Adam, who was with her. He ate it too. And at once, they knew things they had never known before.

One thing they knew was that they were naked! They sewed leaves together to cover themselves.

They'd never felt fear or shame before, so they knew **something was wrong**.

"Adam!" God called. "Eve!"

"We're hiding," said Adam. "We're naked."

"You know that because you ate from the tree." God sighed. Then Adam blamed Eve, and Eve blamed the serpent.

God said, "Serpent, you must crawl on your belly. A woman's son will defeat you. Eve, childbirth will be painful. Adam, growing food will be difficult."

Then God made clothes for Adam and Eve and sent them out of the garden. He put an angel with a flaming sword there, so they could not return.

Sin broke our relationship with God, our loving Creator. But God still loved us. From the start, He had a wonderful plan.

What happened when Adam and Eve ate the fruit?

# TWO BY TWO

## Noah and the Flood

GENESIS 6:5-9:17

The earth filled up with people, but they sinned so much that God was sorry He had made them. He decided to send a flood to wash away everyone on earth.

There was a man named Noah who wasn't like the others. Noah **loved** God and **obeyed** Him. God decided to spare Noah and his family from the flood.

God warned Noah about the flood. He told him to build an enormous boat with a low roof, three decks, a window, and a door.

# IN OBEDIENCE, NOAH BUILT IT.

God told Noah to collect two of every kind of animal. One male. One female. Then Noah, his family, and the animals went into the boat.

# GOD SHUT THE DOOR.

It rained for forty days and forty nights. Water fell from the sky and rose from the oceans and lakes. Even the tallest mountains disappeared beneath the flood.

Meanwhile, Noah, his family, and all the animals were safe in the boat, floating on the flood waters. God had not forgotten about Noah, not even for a moment.

God sent a wind to blow. The waters went down. The boat rested on Mount Ararat. Noah sent out a dove. When it didn't return, he knew it was safe.

When the ground was dry, God told them to come out. He put a rainbow in the sky as a **promise** that He would never flood the whole earth again.

God's wonderful plan was to fix everything broken by sin. His plan continued with Abraham, a man who trusted God.

# GOD'S AMAZING PROMISE

## Abraham Is Called by God

### GENESIS 12:1-9, 15:1-7

Abraham lived in Haran. "Abraham," God said, "I want you to leave Haran and go to another land." God didn't tell Abraham where that was. "**Trust Me**," God said.

"Do this," God said, "and your children will become a great nation!"

"How?" Abraham wondered. His wife, Sarah, was too old to have children.

"**Trust Me**," God said.

"Go where I tell you," God said, "and you will have more descendants than there are stars in the sky! They will bless the whole world. **Trust Me**."

# SO ABRAHAM TRUSTED GOD.

He took Sarah, his nephew Lot, and everything they owned.

He went where God told him to go. He went to the land of Canaan.

When he arrived, Abraham camped at
Shechem.

God appeared to him. "I will give this land
to you and your children," God said. Abraham
built an altar to God there.

Abraham traveled around God's promised land. He was glad that he had trusted God. So he built another altar and gave thanks to God for all he had been promised.

How did Abraham respond to God's amazing promise?

Abraham trusted God to keep His promises, even when those promises seemed impossible. And Abraham trusted God even when God told him to do something really hard.

# ABRAHAM'S BIG TEST

## Abraham and Isaac

GENESIS 15:1-6, 21:1-7, 22:1-19

God promised Abraham a son, and from that son, many descendants, who would bless the whole world. But Abraham and his wife, Sarah, were too old to have children.

Twenty years went by. Still, Abraham trusted God's promise. When he was 100 and Sarah was 90, God reminded them of His promise.

## SARAH WAS GOING TO HAVE A BABY!

When their son was born, Sarah was so joyful that she laughed. "God has brought me laughter!" she said. So they named their son Isaac, which means "he laughs."

When Isaac was a boy, God tested Abraham by telling him to take Isaac to Mount Moriah and kill him as a sacrifice to God. Abraham was confused, but still he trusted God.

Isaac carried the wood, and Abraham held the knife and torch. Together they climbed the mountain. "Where is the lamb for the sacrifice?" asked Isaac.

"God will provide it," Abraham replied.

Abraham arranged the wood on an altar, tied up Isaac, and laid him on the wood. As he raised the knife to kill Isaac, an angel called his name:

"ABRAHAM!"

51

"Don't hurt the boy!" the angel cried. "God knows you trust His promise. Look, there in the bushes! A ram is caught by its horns! Sacrifice that instead."

So Abraham sacrificed the ram instead of his son.

He called the place "God Will Provide" because God provided the sacrifice. Just as God had said.

## HIS PROMISE CAME TRUE.

How did God provide for Abraham?

Isaac had a son named Jacob. God changed Jacob's name to Israel. Israel and his children would play a big role in God's story.

55

# THE DREAMER

## Joseph Is Sold into Slavery

GENESIS 37, 39:1-6

Jacob had twelve sons, but he loved his son Joseph the most. He gave Joseph a special, brightly colored coat. Joseph's brothers were jealous of him. They hated him.

Joseph also had special dreams. "In my dream, we were tying up bundles of wheat," he said. "And your bundles bowed down to mine!" Joseph's brothers hated him even more.

Joseph had another dream. "The sun, the moon, and eleven stars bowed down before me."

His father and brothers grumbled. "Are you saying you will rule over us?"

One day, Joseph's brothers were in the fields watching their sheep. They saw him coming to see them. They planned to kill him and put an end to all his dreams.

"It would be wrong to kill our brother," said
Reuben. "Let's throw him in this empty well." So
they tore off Joseph's special coat and threw
him into the well.

Ishmaelite traders came by on their way to Egypt. "Let's sell Joseph as a slave to the Ishmaelites!" suggested Judah.

So the brothers sold Joseph for twenty pieces of silver.

The brothers dipped Joseph's coat in goat's blood and showed it to Jacob. "My son is dead!" he wept. Meanwhile, Joseph was taken to Egypt.

# BUT GOD WAS WITH JOSEPH.

In Egypt, the Ishmaelites sold Joseph to Potiphar, one of Pharaoh's captains. God blessed Joseph and made him successful. Potiphar put Joseph in charge of his whole household.

What did his brothers do to Joseph?

Joseph honored God by working hard for Potiphar. But God had an even bigger job for Joseph.

# DREAMS COME TRUE

## Joseph's Rise to Power

GENESIS 39-45

Joseph served Potiphar well. Potiphar's wife wanted Joseph to sin against God. Joseph refused, so she lied about him. Potiphar believed her, and Joseph was thrown into prison.

In prison, Joseph met two of Pharaoh's servants. They each had dreams, and God showed Joseph their meaning. Joseph's explanations came true. The cupbearer was released, and the baker was hanged.

Two years later, Pharaoh had two troubling
dreams. The cupbearer remembered what
Joseph had done for him and told Pharaoh.
So Pharaoh sent for Joseph and told him his
dreams.

God showed Joseph the meaning of Pharaoh's dreams. "For seven years, a lot of food will grow," said Joseph. "So store up food because seven years of famine will follow."

Pharaoh was impressed by Joseph's wisdom. So he put Joseph in charge of storing up all the food. Apart from Pharaoh, no one in Egypt was more powerful than Joseph.

Joseph's brothers went to Egypt to buy food. They bowed before Joseph but did not recognize him. When he saw that they had changed, he told them who he was.

# THE BROTHERS WERE TERRIFIED.

"You meant to harm me," Joseph said. "**But God used that for good.** Bring all of our family to Egypt. We will have plenty to eat!"

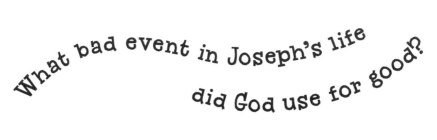

What bad event in Joseph's life did God use for good?

Joseph's father, Israel, and all Israel's children went to the land of Egypt. They lived in Egypt for over four hundred years. God blessed Abraham's descendants, and they grew into a nation of many people.

# A BABY AND A BUSH

## The Birth of Moses and the Burning Bush

EXODUS 1:6-2:15, 3:1-15, 4:1-17

Egypt was filled with Israelites. The new Pharaoh was afraid that the Israelites would become too powerful. So he made them slaves and treated them very badly.

Pharaoh ordered that all baby Israelite
boys had to be killed. One woman put her
baby in a basket and hid him by the river's
edge. His sister watched him.

78

Pharaoh's daughter was bathing by the river. She found the baby and decided to keep him. His sister offered their mother's help to care for him. Pharaoh's daughter named him **Moses**.

Moses grew up. One day he saw an Egyptian beating an Israelite. Moses killed the Egyptian.

Then he fled to Midian and was a shepherd for forty years.

Moses was watching his sheep on Mount Horeb. The voice of God spoke from a **burning bush**. "My people are suffering, Moses. I have chosen you to free them."

"I can't!" Moses cried.

**"I'LL HELP YOU," GOD PROMISED.**

"Throw down your staff," God said. Moses did. It turned into a snake. When he picked it up, it was a staff again.

"Put your hand in your cloak," God said.
Moses did. He looked. It was covered with
disease. When he did it again, it was healed.
"Show Pharaoh that!" God said.

"I'm not a good speaker," said Moses.

"I'll give you the words," God said. "Your brother Aaron can help."

So Moses went to tell Pharaoh to set the Israelites free.

What did God ask Moses to do?

God saw His people. He heard their cries. He was always with them. He remembered His promises to them. And because He loved them, He saved them.

# LET MY PEOPLE GO!

## The Plagues and the Passover

EXODUS 7:14-12:32

Moses and Aaron told Pharaoh, "The God of the Israelites says you must let His people go free. Otherwise, bad things will happen to you."

BUT PHARAOH
WOULD NOT LISTEN.

So God turned the water in Egypt into blood. No one could drink it. Then He filled the Egyptian houses with frogs. Frogs were everywhere!

STILL PHARAOH WOULD NOT LISTEN.

So God filled the skies of Egypt with gnats. They covered the people like dust. Then He struck the land of Egypt with flies.

## STILL PHARAOH WOULD NOT LISTEN.

So God killed the animals of Egypt. Horses, donkeys, camels, sheep, cows, and goats all died. Then He covered the Egyptian people with sores.

## STILL PHARAOH WOULD NOT LISTEN.

God sent hail to crush the crops of Egypt. Their barley and flax were destroyed. Then He sent locusts to eat what fruit remained.

## STILL PHARAOH WOULD NOT LISTEN.

So God sent darkness over the land.

# BUT AGAIN, PHARAOH WOULD NOT LISTEN.

God said, "I will kill every firstborn son in Egypt, and all the firstborn of the animals."

"My people must kill a lamb, eat it, and put its blood on their doorposts. I will see the blood and pass over their houses. Those children will not die."

"You will call this Passover and always remember it." The Israelites obeyed God, but the Egyptian firstborn sons died—even Pharaoh's son.

Why did God strike Egypt with plagues?

# FINALLY, PHARAOH LISTENED.

He let the Israelites go.

God brought His people out of slavery.

He led them with a bright cloud by day
and with a tower of fire by night.

# GOD MAKES A WAY

## The Parting of the Red Sea and the Ten Commandments

EXODUS 14, 16:11-16, 17:1-7, 19-20

After Pharaoh's son died in the tenth plague,
he let the Israelites leave.

They were near the Red Sea when Pharaoh
changed his mind again and chased
after them.

When the Israelites saw Pharaoh's chariots, they were terrified.

But God told Moses to raise his staff toward the Red Sea. God sent a strong wind and parted the sea!

A dry path appeared, and the Israelites
walked straight through the Red Sea. There
was a wall of water on each side of them.

THEY ARRIVED SAFELY
ON THE OTHER SIDE.

Pharaoh and his army followed them into the sea. God told Moses to stretch out his hand.

Then the sea rolled back again, and Pharaoh and his army all drowned.

God led His people through a wilderness. He fed them and gave them water. They camped at Mount Sinai, where God told Moses to meet Him on the mountaintop.

Surrounded by fire and smoke, Moses climbed to the top.

## GOD CAME DOWN TO MEET HIM.

Then God gave Moses the Ten Commandments on two stone tablets:

Don't worship other gods.

Don't make idols.

Treat My name with respect.

Treat the Sabbath day as a special day.

Respect your parents.

Don't murder.

Be loyal to your husband or your wife.

Don't steal.

Don't lie.

Don't envy people or what they own.

Now the people knew how to **obey** God.

How did God show His love to His people?

God instructed His people to build a special box called the Ark of the Covenant. Moses kept the Ten Commandments inside the ark. Even so, God's people disobeyed His commandments, but He still loved them. He took care of them as they lived in the wilderness.

# WATERS PART AND WALLS FALL

## Entering the Promised Land

NUMBERS 13-14; JOSHUA 2-3, 5-6

Moses sent twelve spies into the promised land. Ten of them said, "We will never defeat the people there."

But Joshua and Caleb said, "With God's help, we can do it!"

Frightened, the people believed the ten spies. God said, "Only your children, with Joshua and Caleb, will enter the promised land."

So, after forty years in the desert, **it was time!**

Joshua sent two spies into Jericho. They met a woman called Rahab, who hid them and helped them escape down the wall. They promised to spare her and her family.

The Israelites crossed the Jordan River. The priests went first, carrying the Ark of the Covenant. When their feet touched the river, it stopped flowing! Everyone crossed on dry land.

JERICHO WAS NEXT.

The Lord told Joshua, "For six days, march once around Jericho. Then, on day seven, march around seven times. **Blow trumpets! Shout!** The walls will fall down."

## JOSHUA TRUSTED GOD.

He did what the Lord said, and the walls fell down! They took the city. Rahab was spared. God's people began to take the promised land.

What did God tell Joshua to do?

As long as the Israelites followed God, nothing could stand in their way. They began to take the land of Canaan that God had promised them. God provided for His people and brought others into His story.

# WHEREVER YOU GO

## Ruth

RUTH 1-2, 4:9-17

A famine came to Israel. Elimelech, Naomi, and their sons went to Moab to find food. Elimelech died. The sons married Moabite women, Orpah and Ruth. Then the sons died too.

The three women had no husbands. When the famine in Israel was over, Naomi decided to go home. "Stay in Moab," she said to her daughters-in-law. "It's your home."

Orpah stayed. But Ruth said, "Wherever you go, I will go. Your people will be my people. Your God will be my God." Together, Ruth and Naomi went back to Israel.

It was harvest time in Israel. Naomi told Ruth to gather the bits of grain left behind in a field. The field belonged to Boaz, Elimelech's relative. Boaz approached Ruth.

"You were very kind to Naomi," Boaz said.

"Leaving home must have been hard. May
God bless you." He gave Ruth food and told
his workers to watch over her.

130

Ruth told Naomi what happened. Naomi smiled. "When someone dies, his closest relative cares for his family. That person is their kinsman-redeemer. Boaz is our kinsman-redeemer. Stay close to him!"

So Ruth stayed close to Boaz. He liked her more each day. Boaz bought Elimelech's land

and took care of Naomi and Ruth. Then he married Ruth.

Ruth had a son called Obed. Obed's son was Jesse. Jesse's son was David. And David became Israel's greatest king! So God blessed Ruth just as Boaz had prayed.

How did God take care of Ruth?

134

God sent the nation of Israel leaders to help them love and follow Him. One of the best leaders was Samuel.

# A VOICE IN THE NIGHT

## Samuel Is Called by God

1 SAMUEL 1, 2:11, 3

Hannah was sad because she had no children. She prayed, and God gave her a son, Samuel. She was very grateful, so she gave Samuel to God to serve Him.

Hannah left her little boy at the tabernacle with Eli, the priest. Samuel helped old, blind Eli. He even slept in the tabernacle, while Eli slept in a room nearby.

One night, Samuel heard someone call his name. He got up and ran to Eli. **"Here I am,"** he said.

"I didn't call you," Eli grunted. "Go back to bed."

Samuel crept back to bed. He heard his name again. Samuel ran back to Eli.

"**Here I am**," he said.

"I didn't call you," Eli sighed, sleepily. "Go back to bed."

After Samuel heard the voice a third time, Eli said it was the Lord. "If He calls again," said Eli, "say, 'Speak, Lord, Your servant is listening.'"

So Samuel did.

"Samuel," God said, "can you be My prophet and pass My words faithfully on to My people?"

"I can," said Samuel. And he did, until he was an old man.

God continued to speak to Samuel with messages for His people throughout Samuel's life. When Samuel was old, the Israelites wanted a king like the other nations. Samuel told them that God should be their king, but the Israelites didn't listen.

# STONES, SLINGS, AND GIANT THINGS

## David and Goliath

1 SAMUEL 16-17

Israel's first king was named Saul. King Saul did not obey God. So God said to Samuel, the prophet, "Find a man named Jesse. One of his sons will be the new king."

Samuel found Jesse in Bethlehem. He looked at seven of Jesse's sons. They looked handsome and strong.

"Not them," God said. "I don't care about **looks**. I care about what's in a person's **heart**."

Jesse sent for his youngest son, David, who was tending sheep in the fields. Samuel saw him and God said,

## "HE IS THE ONE!"

So David was anointed the new king.

Some time later, Israel fought the Philistines. A giant Philistine soldier called Goliath challenged

148

the Israelites to send a champion to fight him.

But the Israelites were all too afraid.

David brought food to his brothers in the army. He heard Goliath's challenge and was not afraid. "How dare he defy God's army?" asked David.

## "I WILL FIGHT HIM!"

Surprised, King Saul offered David his armor.
"No," said David. "God helped me kill wild
beasts. He will help me against Goliath too!"
David took five stones and a sling.

"Am I a dog?" Goliath roared. "You send this stick of a boy to fight me!"

"You have a spear," said David.

# "BUT I HAVE THE HELP OF ISRAEL'S GOD!"

David put a stone into the sling and threw it. It struck Goliath's forehead and knocked him down. The Israelites defeated the Philistines. With God's help, David was a hero!

Who helped David bring down Goliath?

David became king. Then there were many kings after David. As time passed, God's people turned away from Him. So God sent prophets to remind the people to worship Him, the one true God.

# FIRE FROM HEAVEN

## Elijah

1 KINGS 16:29-17:1, 18:1, 18:17-39

David became a great king. Then his son Solomon reigned. After Solomon died, God's people had many bad kings. King Ahab was one of the worst. His wife, Jezebel, worshipped the false god, Baal.

Jezebel persuaded Ahab and God's people
to worship Baal too. Because of their sins, God
stopped the rain for several years. Then He sent
His prophet, Elijah, to King Ahab.

"You have disobeyed God and worshipped Baal," Elijah said. "Tell everyone, including the prophets of Baal, to meet me on Mount Carmel."

## "I WILL PROVE WHO THE TRUE GOD IS!"

Everyone gathered on the mountain. Then Elijah said to the people, "Make up your mind! If the Lord is God, follow Him. However, if Baal proves himself today, follow him."

"Baal's prophets and I will each kill a bull, place it on an altar, and pray. The god that sends fire to burn up the bull is the true God!"

Baal's prophets went first. They prayed to Baal all morning. No fire came.

"Maybe Baal is sleeping," Elijah laughed. "Shout louder!" So Baal's prophets shouted all afternoon. Still, nothing happened.

Elijah built an altar. He put the bull and the wood on it. He dug a ditch around it. Then he had water poured over everything until the ditch was full.

Elijah prayed.

# IMMEDIATELY FIRE FELL FROM HEAVEN!

It burned up the bull, the wood, the stones, and the water. The people bowed down and cried, "The Lord is God!"

How did Elijah show the people that the Lord is God?

Sadly, the people didn't listen to the prophets God sent. They worshipped false gods and turned their backs on God's love for them. But God stuck to His plan to use His people to bless the world.

# A ROARING RESCUE

## Daniel and the Lions' Den

DANIEL 1:1-6, 6

God's people disobeyed Him, so He let their enemies take them into captivity. Israel's enemies destroyed Jerusalem and carried away many of the Jews to their own country, Babylon.

Daniel was one of the Jews in Babylon. He trusted God and prayed to Him three times a day. God blessed Daniel, and he became a powerful leader in that country.

Some leaders were jealous of Daniel, so they made a new law. People could only pray to King Darius. Whoever disobeyed would be thrown into a lions' den.

169

Darius agreed.

Daniel still prayed to God and was arrested.
Darius was sad; he liked Daniel. He realized
he'd been tricked but couldn't change the law.
Daniel was thrown to the lions.

The lions roared and crept up to Daniel. Then an angel arrived! It was God who sent him. The angel shut the lions' mouths. Daniel spent the night there, unharmed.

At daybreak, Darius went to see if Daniel was alive. "God sent an angel to save me," Daniel said. The king was thrilled. Daniel was pulled out of the den.

Then King Darius had Daniel's enemies thrown into the den. The lions gobbled them up! King Darius told everyone in his kingdom to honor Daniel's powerful, living God.

# Why was Daniel thrown to the lions?

Many years later, in another land, a
brave woman named Esther trusted and
honored God. She was part of God's
plan to protect His people when they
lived outside the promised land.

# THE BRAVE AND BEAUTIFUL QUEEN

## Esther

ESTHER 2-5, 7, 9:20-22

Esther was the Queen of Persia. Even her husband, King Xerxes, didn't know her secret—Esther was Jewish. Esther's cousin, Mordecai, worked at the palace and looked out for her.

Xerxes' advisor, Haman, received a great reward. He was very proud. Everyone except

Mordecai bowed down to him. Haman was insulted. He vowed to kill Mordecai and all the other Jews too!

Haman told Xerxes that the Jews were dangerous and should die. Xerxes agreed and set a day to kill them.

Mordecai was terrified and sent a message to Queen Esther.

"Change the king's mind," said Mordecai.

"If I go to him without his invitation, he can have me killed," Esther replied.

"Perhaps you were made queen just for this moment," said Mordecai.

## ESTHER BRAVELY AGREED TO TRY.

She went to the throne room. King Xerxes was amazed by her beauty and invited her in. "Can we have dinner with Haman?" she asked.

Haman was building a big gallows in his back yard. He planned to hang Mordecai on it. Then the king's invitation arrived. So Haman went to the palace for dinner.

"A man wants to kill me and my people," Esther told Xerxes.

"Who would do such a thing?" he asked.

"The evil Haman!" Esther cried.

"Haman? Guards! Put him to death."

So Haman was hanged on the gallows he'd built for Mordecai. Because of Esther, the Jews were saved! They celebrated with a great feast, which they observe to this day.

What did Esther do that was brave?

186

After many years, at just the right time, the plan God made at the beginning came true. He sent His only Son, Jesus, to fix people's relationship with God.

# THE FIRST CHRISTMAS GIFT

## Jesus Is Born

LUKE 1:26-38, 2:1-21; MATTHEW 1:18-25

The angel Gabriel told Mary, "You will have a baby!"

"How?" asked Mary. "I'm not married."

"God's Holy Spirit will come down to you. The baby will be God's Son." Mary believed him.

Mary was engaged to Joseph. An angel visited him too. "Mary has done nothing wrong. Her baby will be God's Son. You must name Him Jesus."

Many months passed. Then they traveled to Bethlehem, Joseph's hometown, to be counted by the government.

After that long journey, Mary was ready to give birth.

But all the inns in Bethlehem were full. So God's Son was born in a stable, wrapped in cloths, and laid on a bed of hay.

# THEY NAMED HIM JESUS.

That night, an angel appeared to some shepherds in the hills near Bethlehem. "Good news!" the angel said. "Your Savior has been born. He's in Bethlehem, lying in a manger."

Suddenly more angels appeared, so many of them that they filled the skies.

**"Praise God in heaven!"** they all sang. "And may everyone who pleases Him receive His peace."

When the angels left, the shepherds hurried to Bethlehem.

They found the baby, their Savior, lying on a bed of hay. It was just as the first angel had said.

After the shepherds had seen Jesus, they went through the town. They were very excited! They told everyone what had happened, and they praised God for what He had done!

Jesus grew up. He never sinned, so His relationship with God, His Father, was never broken. Only He could bring people and God back together.

# THE BELOVED SON

## Jesus Is Baptized

MATTHEW 3; LUKE 3:15-22;
JOHN 1:29; MALACHI 3:1

"Before God sends His special Savior," said the prophet Malachi, "a messenger will come to prepare the way for Him." So John came before Jesus, preaching by the Jordan River.

"Prepare the way for the Lord!" John said. "God is sending someone very special to His people. Change your ways. Turn from the bad things you have done. Be baptized."

So that's what people did!

"Are you the promised one?" they asked.

"No," said John. "I'm not worthy to even carry His sandals. He will do amazing things. You'll see!"

Jesus came to John to be baptized. When John saw Jesus, he said, "Behold, the Lamb of God who takes away the sins of the world!"

"I want you to baptize Me," Jesus said.

"No," John replied. "I need to be baptized by You!"

"Trust Me," said Jesus. "This is the right thing to do."

So John baptized Jesus. God's Spirit came down on Jesus like a dove.

**"This is My Son,"** God said. "I love Him. He pleases Me very much!"

Jesus wanted people to understand what their lives would be like if they followed God, loved Him, and trusted Him. Jesus called this "the kingdom of God." It wasn't a kingdom with land and borders. It was a way to live.

How did God show

His love for His Son?

# THE KING AND THE KINGDOM

## The Sermon on the Mount

MATTHEW 4:23–7:29; JOHN 18:36–37

Jesus traveled, teaching about the kingdom of heaven, and crowds followed Him. They didn't know yet that Jesus is the King, but He taught them how to live as people of His kingdom.

"People do good," said Jesus, "because of the good in their hearts. People do evil when evil is in their hearts. God wants to make your heart like His heart."

"Don't worry about things like food and clothes," said Jesus. "Put God first in your life. Obey Him. Trust Him. He will make sure that you have what you need."

Jesus taught this prayer:

*"Father God,*

*Your name is holy.*

*Reign on earth like You reign in heaven.*

*Meet our needs today.*

*Help us obey You."*

## "ALL POWER IS YOURS, FOREVER!"

Then Jesus told a story.

"One man built his house on a rock. A big storm came. Because the house was built on a rock, it did not fall down."

"Another man built his house on soft and shifting sand. A big storm came. Because the house was built on sand, it fell down with a **crash**!"

How can we be like the wise man who built his house on a rock?

"The things I teach you are like the rock," said Jesus. "Put My words into action, and you will be like the man who built his house on a rock."

Everywhere He went, Jesus taught people about God's kingdom, and He healed people from disease and illness. Jesus cared for both people's hearts and their bodies.

# TIME TO GET UP

## Jesus Heals a Girl

LUKE 8:40-42, 8:49-56

Jairus, a leader of the synagogue, fell at Jesus' feet. "My little girl is dying," he cried. "If You lay Your hands on her, I know that she will live."

Pushing through the crowd, they met some men from Jairus's house. "Your daughter is already dead," they said.

"Don't be afraid," said Jesus. "**Believe**, and your daughter will be healed."

They arrived at Jairus's house and found people weeping for the girl. "Why are you weeping?" Jesus asked. "The girl's not dead. She's only sleeping." The people laughed at Him.

Jesus and three of His disciples, Peter, James, and John, went into the house with Jairus and his wife. The little girl was lying there, just as everyone had said.

Jesus took her hand. Then He said,

## "STAND UP, LITTLE GIRL."

And she did! She even walked around the room.

Jairus and his wife were amazed. Jesus told them not to tell anyone what He had done. "Now," said Jesus, "I think this girl needs something to eat!"

How did Jesus help Jairus
and his family?

Jesus healed sick people. He calmed a storm at sea. He walked on water. Through these miracles and more, He showed the people that He was the Savior God sent. In Jesus they saw God's love and power.

# THE BIG PICNIC

## Jesus Feeds Five Thousand People

MARK 6:30-44; JOHN 6:1-15

Jesus had finished teaching. Everyone was hungry. "Send them away to buy food," His disciples said. But Jesus wanted to show the people that they could trust God.

"Why don't you feed them?" Jesus asked.

"It would take a year's wages to buy bread for them all!" His disciples cried.

"How much food do you have?" asked Jesus.

"There is a boy here," said Andrew, "who has five loaves of bread and two little fish."

Jesus smiled. "**Perfect.** Tell the people to sit down on the grass."

So the people sat down all over the mountainside. Jesus thanked God for the bread and the fish. Then He broke them into pieces for His disciples to hand out.

Jesus' disciples passed out bread and fish to the whole crowd. There were five thousand men and lots of women and children too. Everyone ate as much as they wanted.

Afterward the disciples gathered up the leftovers. There were twelve baskets full, from just five loaves and two fish! The people knew they could trust God to care for them.

How did Jesus show the people that they could trust God?

After seeing all the miracles Jesus did, many people wanted Him to be their king. He wasn't like the kings of the world, though. He came as a humble King of a forever kingdom.

# THE DONKEY AND THE KING

## The Triumphal Entry

MATTHEW 21:1-11; LUKE 19:36-40;
JOHN 12:12-19

It was Passover time. Jerusalem was filled with people. When Jesus reached the Mount of Olives, a hill overlooking Jerusalem, He told two of His disciples to find a donkey.

They found the donkey and put their cloaks on it.

Jesus rode on the donkey, fulfilling the Bible verse that says, "Here comes your King, Jerusalem, riding on a donkey."

Jesus rode the donkey down to Jerusalem. Many people remembered His miracles and joined Him. They put cloaks and palm branches on the road before Him to honor Him.

They hoped that Jesus was God's promised Savior.

So they shouted:

## "HOSANNA!"

"Blessed is He who comes in the name of the Lord! Blessed is the King of Israel!"

"The whole world is following Him," the Pharisees grumbled. "Tell them to be quiet, Jesus!"

"Even if everyone stopped shouting," Jesus replied, "the stones would still praise Me!"

# What did the people shout when Jesus came to Jerusalem?

Jesus knew that it was time for Him to leave the world and to go back to His Father. Before He left, He wanted His disciples to know He loved them no matter what.

# A GOODBYE MEAL

## The Last Supper

MATTHEW 26:14-30; MARK 14:10-26;
JOHN 13:26-30

Jesus healed sick people and fed hungry people. He loved outcasts and taught everyone about God's kingdom.

But the religious leaders didn't like His teaching and were jealous of Him.

They hated Jesus so much that they decided to have Him killed.

They gave thirty pieces of silver to Judas, one of Jesus' disciples, to hand Jesus over to them.

Then Jesus and His disciples celebrated the Passover. While they ate, Jesus said sadly, "One of you will betray Me."

Surprised, they each replied, "It's not me, Lord!"

"It's true," said Jesus. "One of you, eating here, will betray Me."

"Not me, Lord," said Judas.

"You know it is," Jesus replied. "Go. Do it quickly!" So Judas left.

Jesus took bread and thanked God for it. He broke it, gave it to His disciples, and said, "**Remember Me** when you eat this. It's My body, given for you."

Then Jesus picked up a cup and thanked God for it. "Everyone drink from this cup," He said. "This is My blood, poured out so that sins may be forgiven."

When they had finished eating, Jesus and His disciples sang a hymn together. Then they walked to the Garden of Gethsemane to pray.

What did Jesus say about the bread and the cup?

Later, the disciples would remember what Jesus told them during this meal. Only then would they understand what Jesus meant when He said, "This is My body, given for you" and "This is My blood, poured out so that sins may be forgiven." Jesus said these things so that His followers would understand what was about to happen.

# IN THE GARDEN

## Jesus Is Arrested

MATTHEW 26:31-75;
JOHN 18:1-8, 18:15-18, 18:25-27

After they ate together, Jesus told His disciples, "Tonight, you will abandon Me."

"Not me!" said Peter boldly. "I will never leave You, Jesus."

Jesus sighed. "Before the rooster crows to greet the morning, you will say, three times, that you don't know Me."

"I'll die with You before I do that!" Peter said.

When they came to the Garden of Gethsemane, Jesus asked His disciples to pray with Him. The disciples were tired. They fell asleep. Jesus prayed alone to the Father.

Jesus knew His enemies wanted Him dead. He also knew that dying was God's plan for Him. "Show Me another way," He prayed. "Otherwise, I will do what You ask."

Suddenly, a light shone. There was shouting, and everyone woke up! An angry crowd approached, sent by the religious leaders. Judas kissed Jesus to show them which man to arrest.

"I'm the one you're looking for," said Jesus. When He said this, they drew back and fell to the ground. Then they grabbed Jesus and took Him to the religious leaders.

Most of Jesus' disciples fled, but Peter followed behind. He waited in a courtyard to see what would happen. "Weren't you with Jesus?" someone asked. Frightened, Peter said, "**No!**"

Two other people asked the same thing. "**You're wrong!**" Peter said. "**I don't even know Jesus!**"

Peter denied Jesus three times. When he heard the rooster crow, he wept bitterly.

What did Jesus want the disciples to do in the garden?

The religious leaders accused Jesus of lying and speaking against God. Jesus did not defend Himself. It was time for Him to complete God's plan.

# IT IS FINISHED!

## The Cross

LUKE 23; JOHN 18:28-19:42

The religious leaders told the governor, Pilate, that Jesus was dangerous and wanted to be king. Pilate asked Jesus, "Is this true?"

**"I am King,"** Jesus answered, "but not of this world."

"Jesus is innocent," said Pilate. "There's no reason to kill Him. I will set Him free."

But the crowd shouted, **"Kill Him!"**

So Pilate had his soldiers whip Jesus. They forced a thorny crown on His head. Then they laid a wooden cross on His back and led Him up a hill.

There on that hill, the Roman soldiers nailed Jesus to the cross, hands and feet. Then they raised it high. Jesus hung there between two criminals.

Around noon, the sky turned dark. Jesus' friends wept. The religious leaders laughed and said, "You saved other people. Why can't You save Yourself?"

"Forgive them, Father," said Jesus.

When the time came for Jesus to die, He closed His eyes and said, **"It is finished."**

He had completed what He had come to do because of His great love.

One of Jesus' followers, a man named Joseph, put Jesus' body in a brand-new tomb. He rolled a huge stone in front of it. A long, sad Friday was over.

Why did Jesus die on the cross?

Jesus' death on the cross was not a defeat. It was God's plan. When Jesus died, He took the punishment for our sins to fix our broken relationship with God. Jesus promised something special would happen on the third day after He died.

# A HAPPY SUNDAY!

## The Empty Tomb

MATTHEW 28:5-8; MARK 16:1-8; LUKE 24:1-12, 24:36-49; JOHN 20:3-10

Sunday morning, some women went to put burial spices on Jesus' body. They knew a big stone was covering the tomb's entrance and wondered how they would move it.

When they arrived, the stone had already been moved. Jesus' body was gone, and there were angels in the tomb!

**"Jesus is alive!"** the angels said. "Go tell His disciples."

The women told the disciples, and Peter and John ran to Jesus' tomb to see for themselves. All they found were Jesus' burial cloths. They went back home, confused.

Later, the disciples were gathered together in a room. They were talking about what had happened when Jesus appeared to them! They were terrified. They thought He was a ghost.

"Don't worry," said Jesus. "See My hands and feet. **It's Me!** Touch Me. Go on. You can't touch a ghost. And ghosts don't eat either, but I'm feeling really hungry."

So He ate some fish. Then He taught them. "The Scriptures are clear," He said. "The Messiah was supposed to suffer and die and then be raised from the dead."

"Now tell the world what you have seen."

"Let everyone know that their sins can be forgiven if they turn to God. It's possible because of what I have done."

Jesus appeared to more than five hundred of His followers over the next forty days and proved that He was actually alive. He also talked to them about the kingdom of God.

# INTO THE CLOUDS

## Jesus Returns to Heaven

MATTHEW 28:18-20; ACTS 1:4-12

It was time for Jesus to go to heaven. He led His disciples to the top of a mountain near Jerusalem. "Here's what I want you to do," He said.

"Wait in Jerusalem until you receive the promised Holy Spirit. Then tell everyone about Me."

"Go from Jerusalem, to Judea, to Samaria, and then to the rest of the world!"

"Make many disciples. Baptize them in the name of the Father, the Son, and the Holy Spirit. Teach them everything you learned from Me. **I will always be with you**."

When He had said this, Jesus rose into the sky.
Up He went until He disappeared into a cloud.
His disciples watched Him. They stood there,
staring into the sky.

Two men, dressed in white, appeared. "Jesus has gone to heaven," they explained. "He will come back in the same way!" So the disciples obeyed Jesus and went to Jerusalem.

What did Jesus tell His disciples to do before He went to heaven?

Before He left, Jesus promised His disciples He would send God's Holy Spirit. The Spirit would help them understand how to live.

# GOD'S WONDERFUL GIFT

## The Holy Spirit Comes

ACTS 2

Jews from all over the world were in Jerusalem for the Feast of Pentecost. Jesus' followers were there too. They gathered together, waiting for the gift Jesus had promised them.

In the middle of the festival, God's gift arrived. It began with a sound, a sound like a howling **wind** that filled the house where they were waiting.

Next, something that looked like **fire** settled on each one of them. Then God's Holy Spirit filled everyone in the room, and He gave them power to speak different languages!

Jews from other parts of the world heard them and were amazed. "These people are speaking our languages," they said, "and proclaiming the wonderful things God has done!"

"This is God's gift," Peter explained. "It was promised long ago. It comes to us through Jesus, the Messiah. You crucified Him, but God brought Him back to life."

"What should we do?" the people asked sadly.

"Turn away from evil," said Peter. "Believe in Jesus Christ. He will forgive your sins and give you His Holy Spirit."

303

On that day, three thousand people were baptized. They were just the first of many people who would come to trust in Jesus as their Savior.

What did Peter say would happen if we believe in Jesus?

When those three thousand people decided to follow Jesus, they became members of God's family, the church. With the Holy Spirit's power, the disciples taught about Jesus and even performed miracles. Many more people believed in Jesus.

# NO SILVER, NO GOLD

## A Crippled Man Is Healed

ACTS 3:1-4, 4

Peter and John went to the temple. A man was there, at the Beautiful Gate, who had never been able to walk. He was begging people for money.

"Can I have some money?" he asked Peter and John. The two disciples looked right at the man. They had no money, but they had something better to give him.

"Look at us!" said Peter. The man expected money. "I don't have any silver or gold," said Peter. "But I have something else that I will happily give you."

"In the name of **Jesus Christ** of Nazareth,"
said Peter, "walk!" Peter took the man's hand,
and the man's feet and ankles grew strong.

## THE MAN GOT UP AND WALKED!

He went with Peter and John into the temple courts. Before long, he wasn't just walking. He was **jumping** around and **praising** God. The people had seen him at the gate. They knew that he had been lame from birth. Yet there he was, walking and leaping and thanking God! Everyone was amazed.

Peter told the people about the One whose power had healed the man. He told them about Jesus. When he was done, many of them decided to follow Jesus too.

What did Peter give the begging man?

God used Peter to lead the new church. Many Jews believed Peter's message about Jesus. But God needed Peter and all the Jews to understand one very important thing about His love.

# EVERYBODY'S WELCOME!

## Peter's Vision and Cornelius

ACTS 10

Cornelius was an officer in the Roman army.
He lived in a place called Caesarea. He and
his family respected God. They weren't Jewish.
They were Gentiles.

Cornelius had a vision. An angel told him, "God hears your prayers and knows that you help the poor. Send men to Joppa to bring Peter here." So Cornelius did.

In Joppa the next day, Peter was on the roof praying. In a vision, a huge sheet came from heaven. It was filled with animals. A voice said, "Kill something, Peter! Eat!"

They were animals that Jews weren't allowed to eat. "I can't eat them," Peter replied.

"If I say they're all right to eat," the voice replied, "then they're all right."

That's when Cornelius's messengers arrived. So Peter and some others went with them to Caesarea.

Cornelius's house was filled with his friends and family, eager to hear Peter speak.

"God showed me, in a vision, that He accepts people from every nation. **God sent Jesus to everyone.** He is Lord of all. He healed the sick and freed the oppressed."

"He was crucified and then raised from the dead. Everyone who believes in Him will be forgiven of their sins."

The Holy Spirit came upon them, just like Pentecost. Peter baptized them.

Who did God send Jesus to?

Jesus' disciples spread the news about Him in Israel. But God wanted His good news of salvation to go to everyone. God knew the right man for the job.

# FROM ENEMY TO FRIEND

## Saul Meets Jesus

330

Saul was a religious man, a Pharisee. He
thought that anyone who believed in Jesus was
spreading a lie and should be put in prison,
and even put to death.

Saul was going to Damascus to arrest Jesus' followers. Suddenly a bright light surrounded him. He fell down.

A voice said, **"Saul, why are you so cruel to Me?"**

"Who are You, Lord?" Saul asked.

The voice replied, **"I am Jesus**, the one you want to harm. Go to Damascus. There you will learn what you must do."

Saul got up, but he was blind. His friends led him to a house in Damascus. Saul waited there for three days. He had nothing to eat or drink.

Meanwhile Jesus appeared in a vision to Ananias, one of His followers in Damascus. Jesus told him to go visit Saul and pray for him so he could see again.

337

"But Saul wants to arrest Your followers," Ananias said, trembling.

"I know," said Jesus. "But I want to use Saul

to tell people all over the world about Me."

Ananias went to pray for Saul. "Jesus sent me," he said, "so that you may see and be filled with the Holy Spirit."

Saul could see again! Then he was baptized.

Jesus changed Saul from a man who hurt His followers to a church leader who told everyone about Jesus!

What was different in Saul's life after he met Jesus?

342

God told Saul to share the good news of Jesus
with the Gentiles, people who are not Jewish.
These people spoke the Greek language,
so they called him Paul, which is Greek
for Saul. Paul would face many challenges
as he worked to tell people about Jesus.

# JOURNEYS FOR JESUS

## Paul's Journeys and Trials

ACTS 13-14, 16-21, 25, 27-28

Paul believed that God wanted him to tell Gentiles about Jesus. So he made three trips through Syria, Turkey, and Greece. Many people believed in Jesus, and many churches were started.

Years later, Paul returned to Jerusalem.
Some people were upset by his teaching
and attacked him. He was unfairly arrested.

Since Paul was a Roman citizen, he
asked for his trial to be in Rome.

Paul was put on a boat headed for Rome. The trip was slow. "Let's wait in Crete until the stormy season is over," Paul suggested. The captain sailed ahead anyway.

There was a huge storm. Everyone thought they would die. An angel told Paul that they would all be saved, and he would get to Rome. Paul told the others.

Someone spotted land. The sailors planned to abandon ship and let the others die. Paul warned: "You will survive only if everyone stays aboard." The boat crashed on an island called Malta.

The soldiers were afraid of being punished if the prisoners escaped. So they decided to kill them. But their commander liked Paul, so he ordered his men to let them live.

They staggered ashore. Just as Paul had said, everyone was alive! The ruler of Malta let them stay with him. His father was sick. When Paul prayed for him, God healed him.

They boarded another ship and went to
Rome, where Paul was chained in a house.
While there, he wrote letters to teach the new
churches around the world. His letters are now
included in the Bible!

What did Paul do
when he was a
prisoner in Rome?

By the same power that brought Jesus back
from the dead, God will one day make all
things new. Jesus will return just like God's
Word promises, and those who believe
in Jesus will live with Him forever.

# A FOREVER PROMISE

## The New Heaven and the New Earth

REVELATION 1:10-19, 20:7-10, 21:1-7

John was a disciple of Jesus. One day
Jesus came to him in a vision, shining like
the sun. "Don't be afraid," said Jesus.
"I died. Now I live forever!"

Then John saw a new heaven and a new earth, God's promised new creation. The first heaven and the first earth were gone and the sea with them.

Next John saw God's Holy City, the new
Jerusalem. It was coming down from heaven.
It was beautiful, like a bride on her wedding
day ready to meet her husband.

Then John heard a loud voice coming from the throne of God saying, "From now on, God will make His home among His people, and they will all live together."

"In this new heaven and new earth, there won't be any tears because no one will be in pain, and no one will die. Those things are gone forever!"

362

Then the voice from the throne said, "I am the Beginning and the End. If you are thirsty, come to Me, and I will give you the water of life."

"My new world is for My children, those who are faithful to Me. **I'm making all things new.** It's true. You can count on it."

What are you looking forward to in the new world God promises?

Jesus showed John many things about heaven and the new creation. They were beautiful!

# GOD'S GOOD NEWS

## Be Part of the Story

# IN THE BEGINNING, GOD MADE EVERYTHING.

He made it perfect. He made us, too, in His image. He loves us and wants to have a relationship with us.

Sadly, Adam and Eve disobeyed God. That
sin brought death into the world and broke
our relationship with God. It also broke God's
perfect world.

Sin spread throughout the whole world.

Everyone sins, and the result of sin is death.

But sin couldn't stop God from loving us.

## HE HAD A PLAN!

Because of His love for us, God sent His Son,
Jesus, into the world. Sin broke our relationship
with God, but Jesus came to fix it!

Jesus healed sick people and performed many other miracles.

He welcomed lonely people. He taught people about God's love. His perfect life shows us what love looks like.

Even though Jesus never sinned, He died on a cross for our sins because He loves us. By doing this, He was carrying out God's plan to fix our relationship with Him.

Three days later, Jesus rose from the dead, breaking the power of sin and death! He spent time with His followers, teaching them. Then He returned to heaven.

## NOW JESUS LIVES FOREVER!

Jesus did not leave us alone. He sent His Holy Spirit to live inside everyone who trusts Him. The Spirit gives us power to live the way God created us to live.

One day, when Jesus returns, God will make everything **perfect** again. He will make a new heaven and a new earth. Everyone who trusts in Jesus will live with Him, forever!

GOD LOVES YOU.

He created you one-of-a-kind! Trusting and following Jesus fixes our broken relationship with God.

Are you ready to be a part of God's story?

# Continue the Journey...

You've reached the end of this book, but God's Story is not over! There is so much more to learn! All the stories you've just read are part of an app called the *Bible App for Kids*. Get the FREE interactive app!

## What is the *Bible App for Kids*?

Created by YouVersion and OneHope, the *Bible App for Kids* is sharing God's Story with children around the world.

You can view the stories in this book, as well as many more. All Bible stories are animated with music, narration, and fun activities!

It is the most-downloaded children's Bible app of all time.

Available in many languages, the app is regularly updated to reach even more kids around the world in their heart language.

# BibleAppforKids.com

FREE resources for parents are available so your whole family can engage with the app, as well as a Sunday School curriculum so your church can get involved! Resources include

- Video Episodes
- Family Devotionals
- Coloring Pages
- Activity Sheets

- *Bible App for Kids* Curriculum
  - Original, downloadable songs
  - Live-action hosts
  - Animated characters
  - Memory verses with motions
  - Leader training video

## Download the FREE interactive app

The Bible App for Kids • bible.com/kids

## YouVersion

YouVersion helps you engage with the Bible through free apps like the *Bible App* and the *Bible App for Kids*. Whether you're a frequent or first-time reader of the Bible, the apps give you a meaningful experience in God's Word without the interruption of ads. YouVersion is a ministry of Life.Church, a multi-site church based in Oklahoma. Meeting in locations throughout the United States and globally online at live.Life.Church, our church is devoted to leading people across the planet to become fully devoted followers of Christ. Get the world's most popular Bible app at bible.com/app and visit bible.com/kids to download the free *Bible App for Kids*.

OneHope is an international ministry that reaches children and youth around the world with God's Word—more than 1.5 billion kids in 145 countries have encountered a OneHope Scripture program since 1987! By collaborating with thousands of local churches and ministries, local governments, schools, and non-governmental organizations, OneHope plans to reach every child with God's Word. onehope.net

An Imprint of Thomas Nelson
thomasnelson.com